G000071391

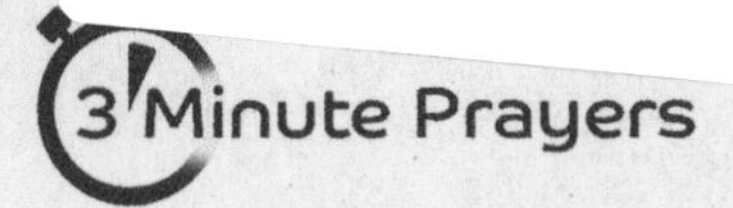
3 Minute Prayers

kevin
mayhew

kevin
mayhew

First published in Great Britain in 2019 by Kevin Mayhew Ltd
Buxhall, Stowmarket, Suffolk IP14 3BW
Tel: +44 (0) 1449 737978 Fax: +44 (0) 1449 737834
E-mail: info@kevinmayhew.com

www.kevinmayhew.com

9 8 7 6 5 4 3 2 1 0

ISBN 978 1 84867 981 8
Catalogue No. 1501601

Cover design by Rob Mortonson

Typeset by Angela Selfe

Printed and bound in Great Britain

CONTENTS

ABOUT THE AUTHOR

Nicky would describe herself as mainly a mum, but she finds time, between school runs, to volunteer at her local Citizens Advice Bureau. She is also the Prayer Co-ordinator for MissionAssist and writes a monthly 'Thought' to encourage people in their faith. Once school is out, Nicky is kept busy helping with homework, music practice and catching up with the events of the day, but there's still plenty of time for family games and movies.

Nicky always has a book on the go and enjoys reading historical fiction that gives a glimpse of how people used to live and how society has changed. The mountains have

always had restorative powers for Nicky, reminding her of the greatness of our creator God. Having recently bought a bicycle, she is discovering the joy of cycling near her home on the edge of the New Forest.

Having grown up in a loving Christian family, Nicky now, along with husband Graham, encourages her two daughters, Lucy and Sophie, to discover more about Jesus and the difference that knowing him can make to their lives.

In this book Nicky wants to give words to children that they can use to speak to Jesus, and to give them the confidence to speak words of their own as they grow in relationship with him.

INTRODUCTION

Sometimes it's hard to know how to pray. Are there special words I should use? Do prayers have to be long? Can I only pray in church, before meals and at bedtimes? Does Jesus really want to hear from me?

This book is full of prayers for different situations you might find yourself in at home and school. There are also some questions to help you think through things that have happened and how to move forward, so that you can grow more into the person Jesus wants you to be.

I have two daughters myself and I have used these ideas to help them to learn to pray and to grow in confidence, so that they can talk to Jesus about anything and everything.

By using the prayers in this book yourself, you will discover that Jesus does want to know about your life and that what is important to you, is important to him. The easy language I use should help you to continue praying and expand the prayers yourself, such that you are talking freely to Jesus about your life and family. You'll also find that even in tricky situations there can be things to be thankful for and the Bible verse with each prayer will encourage you as you move forward.

You might like to use a mix of prayers and then add something yourself, whether that's praying for a particular person or praying about something that is going on in your life, your family, or the world.

Whether you use these prayers at bedtime or a different time of day, Jesus is longing to hear from you and wants to be a part of your everyday life.

MY SCHOOL

1 NEW TEACHER

What is my teacher's name?

What do I like about my teacher?

How can I help my teacher?

PRAYER

Dear Jesus,
I've got a new teacher.
I'm not sure what they'll be like.
I hope they're not shouty
but will be kind and help me to learn.

Thank you that you give us lots of people who
help us to learn all about the world you made
and to help us to grow up
to be the best we can be.
Amen

BIBLE VERSE

Pay attention to your teacher
and learn all you can.

Proverbs 23:12

2 NEW SCHOOL

What is my new school called?

How will I get to school?

How can I make new friends?

PRAYER

Dear Jesus,
I'm about to start a new school!
Will I find my way?
Will I know where to find things?
Will I have a friend in my class?
Will I make new friends?
Will the work be hard?

Thank you that you listen to all my worries
and that you care about how I feel.
Please help me not to worry
about these things.
Amen

BIBLE VERSE

Intelligent people are always
eager and ready to learn.

Proverbs 18:15

3 FALLING OUT

Who is my friend?

What could I have done differently?

How can I show them I care?

PRAYER

Dear Jesus,
I fell out with my best friend today.
The words came out all wrong.
I tried to make it right, but they just walked away.
I don't know how to make it better.

Thank you that you can show us
the right way to live.
Please help me to speak kindly to my friend
and to show them how much
they mean to me.
Amen

BIBLE VERSE

A gentle answer quietens anger,
but a harsh one stirs it up.

Proverbs 15:1

4 FRIEND OFF SCHOOL

Who are my other friends?

How can I be friendly to others?

How can I make new friends?

PRAYER

Dear Jesus,
my best friend wasn't there today.
I was all alone at work and play.
The empty seat reminded me
of just how much they mean to me.

Thank you that you're always there,
right with me, and that you care.
Help me to be a friend to all,
even when my best friend
is at school.
Amen

BIBLE VERSE

Remember that I have commanded you to be determined and confident! Don't be afraid or discouraged, for I, the Lord your God, am with you wherever you go.

Joshua 1:9

SUCCESS

What is my success?

How long was I trying to succeed?

How did I succeed?

PRAYER

Dear Jesus,
I did it!
I tried and tried my best
and my effort was rewarded
with a good mark in my test.

Thank you for my brain,
and all that it can do.
Help me to follow in your ways
and be a success for you, too.
Amen

BIBLE VERSE

Ask the Lord to bless your plans, and you will be successful in carrying them out.

Proverbs 16:3

6 DISAPPOINTMENT

What was I disappointed with?

What could I have done differently?

What am I good at?

PRAYER

Dear Jesus,
I didn't do very well today.
It feels as though everyone else did better than me
and I feel really disappointed.
I tried my best but it still went wrong.

Please help me to remember that
everyone is good at something
and that you have given me
things to be good at.
Amen

BIBLE VERSE

So we are to use our different gifts
in accordance with the grace that
God has given us.

Romans 12:6

7 TESTS

What tests do I have to do?

How can I prepare for them?

How important are they?

PRAYER

Dear Jesus,
I have tests coming up at school.
We're doing lots of practice;
sometimes I do ok, sometimes I don't.
I know these tests aren't so important,
I'm trying not to make them bigger than they are
but I want to do well.

Help me to see that doing my best is what matters
and whatever the outcome on the day,
thank you that you see me as a complete person
and there's much more to
me than test results.

Amen

BIBLE VERSE

Whatever you do, work at it with all your
heart, as though you were working for
the Lord and not for human beings.

Colossians 3:23

8 SCHOOL TRIPS

Where am I going?

What will I be doing?

What am I hoping to learn?

PRAYER

Dear Jesus,
I'm excited to be going on a
school trip tomorrow.

Thank you that we can go to special places to learn more about how the world you made works. Please help me to make the most of this opportunity and keep being interested in everything that I see and learn.

Amen

BIBLE VERSE

The Lord will guard you;
he is by your side to protect you.

Psalm 121:5

9 THINGS I LIKE

What do I enjoy doing most?

How can I share this with others?

What else do I think I'd like to do?

PRAYER

Dear Jesus,
at school I love . . . . . .

Thank you that I have found something that I enjoy.
Please help me to keep growing my interest in this.
Please help me to encourage others to like this too.

Amen

BIBLE VERSE

Be thankful in all circumstances. This is what God wants from you in your life in union with Christ Jesus.

1 Thessalonians 5:18

10 THINGS I FIND HARD

What do I find hard?

Who can help me if I need it?

How can I keep going?

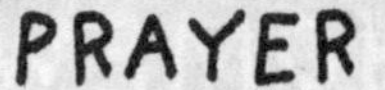

PRAYER

Dear Jesus,
I find . . . . . . really hard.
When I look at the page,
it just doesn't make sense
and I can't work out what to do.

Please help me to try my best
even though I find it hard,
and to ask for help when I need it.
Amen

BIBLE VERSE

I have the strength to face all conditions
by the power that Christ gives me.

Philippians 4:13

11 HOMEWORK

What kind of homework do I have?

How long am I going to spend on it?

What can I look forward to doing when it's done?

PRAYER

Dear Jesus,
I'm at school all day, working really hard,
then I have to do homework too.
I'd much rather be playing and having fun
than sitting doing more work.

Please help me to concentrate on my homework
so I can get it done in good time
and still have time for all the
other things I want to do too.
Amen

BIBLE VERSE

But the Lord stayed with me
and gave me strength.

2 Timothy 4:17

12 LEAVING SCHOOL

Which school am I leaving?

What is a favourite memory from this school?

What am I looking forward to next?

PRAYER

Dear Jesus,
I'm leaving my school!
I've done so much here.
I've learnt so much here.
Everyone knows me
and I know all of them.
So many memories.
It feels sad to be moving on,
but I'm also excited about what comes next.

Thank you that you're always with me,
and you'll be there
whatever comes next.
Amen

BIBLE VERSE

Don't worry about anything, but in all
your prayers ask God for what you need,
always asking him with a thankful heart.

Philippians 4:6

MY FAMILY

I DAD

What do I like about my dad?

What do I like to do with my dad?

What could I do for my dad?

PRAYER

Dear Jesus,
my dad goes out to work all day.
Sometimes he's back late, so he misses tea.
Sometimes he's back so late that he misses bedtime.
But when he is at home, I like to play games with him.

Thank you for the hard work my dad does.
Thank you for the time I spend with my dad.
Help me to make the most of the time
we have together.
Amen

BIBLE VERSE

Above everything, love one another earnestly, because love covers over many sins.

1 Peter 4:8

2 MUM

What do I like about my mum?

What do I like to do with my mum?

What could I do for my mum?

PRAYER

Dear Jesus,
sometimes my mum annoys me because she doesn't listen and understand what I'm feeling.
I get frustrated and she shouts more.

I do love my mum.
I thank you for all that she does for me.
Help me to remember to be kind to her and show her how much she means to me.
Amen

BIBLE VERSE

I thank my God for you
every time I think of you.

Philippians 1:3

3
OLDER SISTER

Who is my older sister (or brother!)?

What could we do together?

How could I show her I love her?

PRAYER

Dear Jesus,
my big sister gets to stay up later.
She gets to watch different things on TV.
She doesn't want to play with me any more.

Please help me to keep loving my big sister
and to understand that things change as we get older.
Please help us to find something we
can do together
so we can grow up to
be good friends.
Amen

BIBLE VERSE

Dear friends, let us love one another, because love comes from God. Whoever loves is a child of God and knows God.

1 John 4:7

YOUNGER BROTHER

Who is my younger brother (or sister!)?

What could we do together?

What could I teach him?

PRAYER

Dear Jesus,
my little brother was annoying me today.
I was trying to play but he kept knocking things over
and getting in the way.

Please help me to be patient with him
and to show him the right way to do things.
Please help me to spend time with him
and help me to be
a good example.
Amen

BIBLE VERSE

Be always humble, gentle, and
patient. Show your love by being
tolerant with one another.

Ephesians 4:2

What is the baby's name?

When is their birthday?

How could I help my mum with the new baby?

PRAYER

Dear Jesus,
there's a new baby in the house!
It's quite noisy sometimes and it
can smell really bad too!
But I like their tiny fingers and toes.

Please help me to be a good big brother/sister.
Help me to find ways I can help
my mum and dad too.
And helps us all as we get used
to having one more in our family.
Amen

BIBLE VERSE

Children are a gift from the Lord;
they are a real blessing.

Psalm 127:3

6 TWO HOMES

What do I like about having two homes?

What do I find hard?

How can I live well in both places?

PRAYER

Dear Jesus,
it can be hard going between two homes;
thank you there are people who
love me in both places.
Sometimes the rules are different.
Help me to respect the rules in each home.
Sometimes it feels I don't belong in either place.

I know you love me no matter what
and you are always the same.
Thank you for all my family.
Amen

BIBLE VERSE

Respect your father and your mother,
so that you may live a long time in
the land that I am giving you.

Exodus 20:12

Who is my family?

What do we fall out about?

How can I show love and kindness to my family?

PRAYER

Dear Jesus,
when my family all get along with each other,
everyone is a bit happier.
Sometimes we fall out
and things feel tense and sometimes scary.

Please help us all to show love
and kindness to each other
and to quickly make up again
if we fall out.
Amen

BIBLE VERSE

Do everything possible on your part
to live in peace with everybody.

Romans 12:18

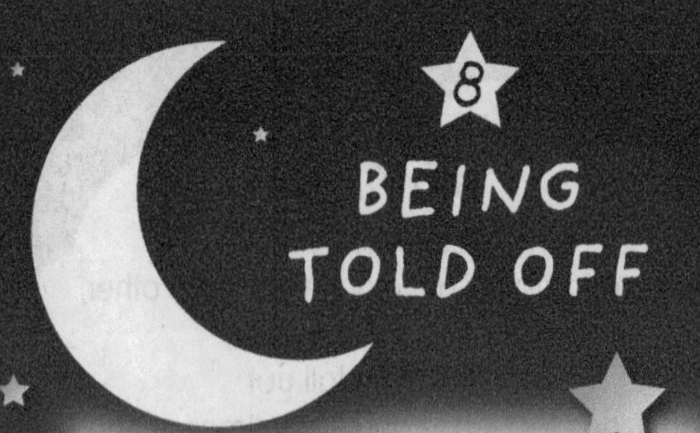

8 BEING TOLD OFF

Who has told me off?

What did I do?

How can I make up for my bad choice?

PRAYER

Dear Jesus,
I hate being told off.
It makes me feel alone.

Sometimes I've done it on purpose,
sometimes by accident,
but either way, I'm told off.
I'm expected to know better.
And deep down I do.

Help me to make better choices
so I can avoid being told off.
Amen

BIBLE VERSE

A wise son pays attention when his father corrects him, but an arrogant person never admits he is wrong.

Proverbs 13:1

9 TEMPTATION

What was I tempted to do?

Who do I need to tell?

How can I avoid giving in to this temptation again?

PRAYER

Dear Jesus,
I know I shouldn't do it
but I want to give it a go.
If I wait till Mum and Dad aren't here,
maybe no one will know.

Help me, please, not to give in,
but make the right choice here.
I know deep down what I should do,
so help me do it here.
Amen

BIBLE VERSE

Keep watch and pray that you will not fall into temptation. The spirit is willing, but the flesh is weak.

Matthew 26:41

10 GROWING UP

What do I like about growing up?

What worries me about growing up?

Who can I talk to?

PRAYER

Dear Jesus,
some days I just want to be older
and bigger
and taller
and faster.

Please help me to enjoy every day
and to look forward to growing up well.

Help me not to be too impatient
but to know that I will grow
up in your perfect time.
Amen

BIBLE VERSE

Everything that happens in this world
happens at the time God chooses.

Ecclesiastes 3:1

MY LIFE

I THANK YOU

What am I thankful for?

Who do I need to thank?

How can I show that I am thankful?

PRAYER

Dear Jesus,
you give us so many good things.

Thank you for the sun to brighten our day.
Thank you for the rain to help things grow.
Thank you for my friends and family
who love and care.

Thank you for . . . . . .

Thank you that you love me.
Amen

BIBLE VERSE

In the name of our Lord Jesus
Christ, always give thanks for
everything to God the Father.

Ephesians 5:20

2 SORRY

What do I need to say sorry for?

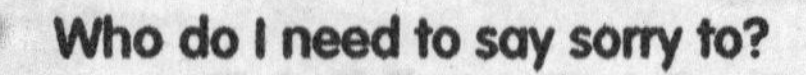

Who do I need to say sorry to?

How can I learn to say sorry more?

PRAYER

Dear Jesus,
sometimes I find it really hard to say sorry.
Why do I have to be first?

Sometimes I'm cross
and I don't want to say sorry.
Other times it flies out of my mouth
and I don't always mean it.

I know it's really important to learn to say sorry.
Please help me to say sorry
when I need to
and to really mean it.
Amen

BIBLE VERSE

Live in peace with one another.

Mark 9:50

Who do I need to forgive?

How can I show them I have forgiven them?

Do I need to ask someone to forgive me?

PRAYER

Dear Jesus,
sometimes when someone says sorry to me,
I don't want to say it's ok and forgive them.
Sometimes I'm hurting.
Sometimes I'm sad.
Sometimes I'm just too cross.

Thank you that you forgive me every
time I do the wrong thing.
Please help me to forgive
other people too.
Amen

BIBLE VERSE

Be tolerant with one another and forgive one another whenever any of you has a complaint against someone else. You must forgive one another just as the Lord has forgiven you.

Colossians 3:13

4 HAPPY

What am I happy about?

What has led to this?

How can I share my happiness with others?

PRAYER

Dear Jesus,
I feel so happy!
Everything's going well:
my life is a happy place.
I have no worries,
I have no cares,
and I know you are there.
Thank you for all the good things you give me
to make my life special
and happy.
Amen

BIBLE VERSE

When people are happy, they
smile, but when they are sad,
they look depressed.

Proverbs 15:13

5 EXCITED

What am I excited about?

How does it make me feel?

How can I relax and go to sleep?

PRAYER

Dear Jesus,
I'm so excited I'm sure I won't sleep!
I feel like there are bubbles inside me
bouncing around and keeping me awake.

Thank you for the variety in my life.
Thank you for this excitement about . . . . . .
Thank you for all the good things you give us.
Amen

BIBLE VERSE

This is the day of the Lord's victory;
let us be happy, let us celebrate!

Psalm 118:24

6 GRIEF

Who has died?

What makes me feel so sad?

What memories do I have?

PRAYER

Dear Jesus,
someone I love has died.
Every time I think of them I feel so sad.
I'm sad because I won't see them again.

Thank you that I won't feel sad forever.
Thank you for all the good times I had with . . . . . .
Please help me to keep those memories special.
Thank you that you understand how I feel.
Amen

BIBLE VERSE

Happy are those who mourn;
God will comfort them!

Matthew 5:4

7 THINGS

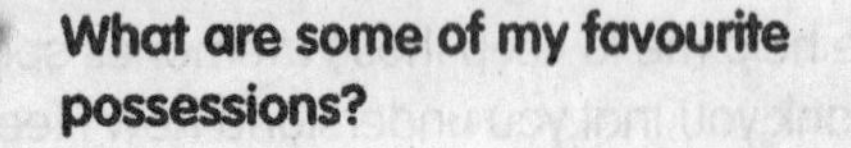

What are some of my favourite possessions?

What do I have that I don't need any more?

Who could I consider giving it to?

PRAYER

Dear Jesus,
I've noticed that some people have more things and some people have fewer.
And that sometimes people are unkind because of what someone has or doesn't have.

Thank you for all the things I have.
Please help me to be satisfied with what I have and not always want more.
Amen

BIBLE VERSE

Do not store up riches for yourselves here on earth, where moths and rust destroy, and robbers break in and steal.

Matthew 6:19

8 WAITING PATIENTLY

What am I waiting for?

How long will I have to wait?

What could I do while I wait?

PRAYER

Dear Jesus,
I don't like waiting.

Waiting at the doctor,
waiting for the bus,
waiting for my birthday,
trying not to make a fuss.

Help me, please, dear Jesus,
to enjoy what I have now,
to see the things around me,
and wait patiently somehow.
Amen

BIBLE VERSE

But if we hope for what we do not see,
we wait for it with patience.

Romans 8:25

What do I want to achieve?

What am I doing to try to achieve it?

What else could I do?

PRAYER

Dear Jesus,
even though I'm small, there are
things I want to do and achieve.
Thank you for giving me ideas and inspiration.
Help me to be determined to do what I plan.
Help me to be brave if there are
bumps along the way.
Amen

BIBLE VERSE

Let us run with determination
the race that lies before us.

Hebrews 12:1

What am I persevering with?

What successes have I had so far?

How can I keep believing I'll get there?

PRAYER

Dear Jesus,
thank you that you are with me in everything I do.
You know how hard I am trying at the moment.
But each time I just don't quite get there.

When I don't succeed, please give
me strength to persevere.
When I feel like giving up, help me to try again.
When I feel I'll never get there,
help me to believe I will.
Amen

BIBLE VERSE

Happy are those who remain
faithful under trials.

James 1:12

11 TIRED

What has made me so tired?

What can I think about while I fall asleep?

What do I look forward to tomorrow?

PRAYER

Dear Jesus,
I'm so tired.
My brain won't think straight.
My legs feel like jelly.
My eyes just want to close.

Thank you for my comfy bed.
Thank you for night time.
Please give me the rest I need
so I'm ready for a new
day tomorrow.
Amen

BIBLE VERSE

Come to me, all of you who are
tired from carrying heavy loads,
and I will give you rest.

Matthew 11:28

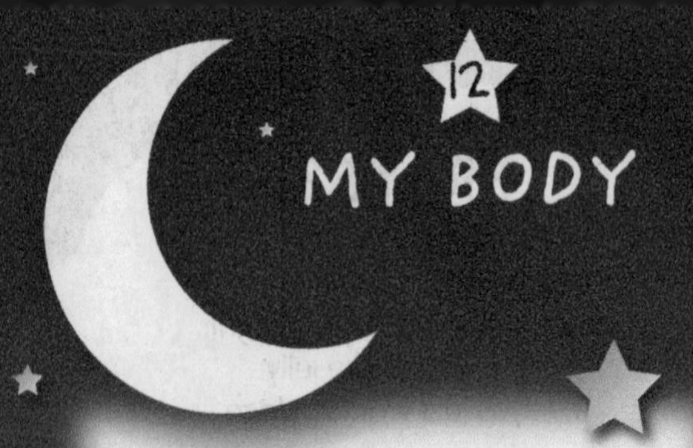

12 MY BODY

What amazing things can my body do?

Have I hurt a part of my body?

How can I look after my body to keep it healthy?

PRAYER

Dear Jesus,
thank you for my body.
Thank you for the amazing way
all the different parts work.
Thank you that it grows without me doing anything.
Thank you for the way my body can heal itself
if part of it is hurt or broken.

Please help me to look after my body
and keep it fit and healthy.
Amen

BIBLE VERSE

You created every part of me; you put
me together in my mother's womb.

Psalm 139:13

MY CHARACTER (FRUIT OF THE SPIRIT)

The Spirit produces love, joy, peace, patience, kindness, goodness, faithfulness, humility, and self-control. There is no law against such things as these.

Galatians 5:22, 23

I LOVE

Who loves me?

How do I know this?

How can I show I love them too?

PRAYER

Dear Jesus,
thank you for the people who love me
no matter what,
for my family and friends.
Help me to show how much I love them too.

Some people I don't like so much.
I know you love them
just like you love me
and want me to love them too.
Please show me how.
Thank you most of all
that you love me.
Amen

BIBLE VERSE

My commandment is this: love
one another, just as I love you.

John 15:12

2 JOY

What is giving me joy today?

How can I try to keep being joyful?

Who could I share my joy with?

PRAYER

Dear Jesus,
some things make me happy,
some things make me grumpy.
It's easy to be happy when the sun's shining
and I'm playing with my friends.
It's easy to moan when I have to tidy my room.

Please help me to be joyful
whether I'm having fun
or doing something I don't want to.
Amen

BIBLE VERSE

Today is holy to our Lord,
so don't be sad.

Nehemiah 8:10

What am I worrying about?

How can I feel calm and peaceful about it?

Who can I talk to about my worries?

PRAYER

Dear Jesus,
sometimes I worry about things:
about my friends and family,
about my school,
if I haven't got the latest toys or clothes.

Help me to be content with what I have
and enjoy what I've been given.
Thank you for your peace,
that you can help me to feel calm,
whatever's going on.
Amen

BIBLE VERSE

May the Lord himself, who is our
source of peace, give you peace
at all times and in every way.

2 Thessalonians 3:16

4 KINDNESS

Who has been kind to me?

Who could I show kindness to?

How could I show kindness?

PRAYER

Dear Jesus,
I like it when people are kind to me.

Please show me opportunities to be
kind to other people.

Maybe I could look out for people in the playground
who have no one to play with,
so I can ask them to play with me.

Or perhaps I could say nice things to encourage
people who might be feeling down.

Thank you for all the people
who show me kindness.

Amen

BIBLE VERSE

Be kind and tender-hearted
to one another.

Ephesians 4:32

5 GOODNESS

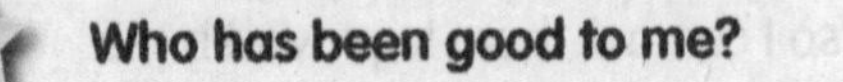

Who has been good to me?

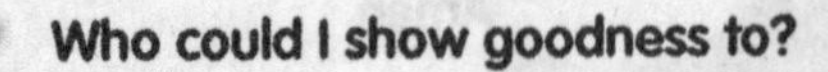

Who could I show goodness to?

How could I show goodness?

PRAYER

Dear Jesus,
thank you that you give us brains
to help us make choices
about how we behave.

Help me to make good choices.
Help me to be a good, loyal friend,
caring and understanding,
so that people can depend on me.
Thank you that you are always good
and always do the
right thing for us.
Amen

BIBLE VERSE

So let us not become tired
of doing good.

Galatians 6:9

6 FAITHFULNESS

How is God faithful to me?

Who am I faithful to?

How can I show this?

PRAYER

Dear Jesus,
thank you that you are faithful to me.
Thank you that you never leave me.
Thank you for all the promises you make in the Bible.
Thank you that you always keep your promises.

Please help me to be loyal to my friends and family.
Please help me to keep promises I make.
Amen

BIBLE VERSE

The Lord is faithful to his promises;
and he is merciful in all his acts.

Psalm 145:13

7 GENTLENESS

Who has been gentle to me?

Who could I show gentleness to?

How could I show gentleness?

PRAYER

Dear Jesus,
it's not always easy to be gentle.
When people shout I shout back.
When people push I push back.
Sometimes my feelings are hurt
if a friend hasn't been gentle to me.

Thank you that you are always gentle.
Please help me to be gentle
and think of other
people's feelings.
Amen

BIBLE VERSE

Be peaceful and friendly, and always show
a gentle attitude towards everyone.

Titus 3:2

When did I not show self-control?

How could I show self-control?

Who can I be a good example to?

PRAYER

Dear Jesus,
I'm sorry for the times I do or say
things I know I shouldn't.

I know I need to be in control of myself,
and of things I say and do.

Thank you for all the thoughts and feelings you give me.
Please help me to use them carefully,
and to think before I speak and act,
so that I can be a good
example to others.
Amen

BIBLE VERSE

Be alert, stand firm in the faith, be brave,
be strong. Do all your work in love.

1 Corinthians 16:13, 14

ACCEPTING DIFFERENCES

What are some differences between me and my friends?

How can I show I love them even though we are different?

Do I need to say sorry to anyone for judging them?

PRAYER

Dear Jesus,
some days I really notice the differences
between me and my friends.
Some are taller,
some are cleverer,
some are faster.

Please help me to love and accept
people for who they are
and not just for how they look
or what they're good at.

Thank you that you made all of us
and that you love all of us too.
Amen

BIBLE VERSE

Love your neighbour as
you love yourself.

Matthew 22:39

10 GOD'S LOVE

How do I know God loves me?

What do I need to say sorry to God for?

How can I show God's love to others?

PRAYER

Dear Jesus,
thank you that you love me.
Thank you that you love me no matter what.

Thank you that even I if I make a
mistake and do the wrong thing,
I can say sorry and you will forgive me.

Help me to remember how
precious I am to you.
Amen

BIBLE VERSE

For God loved the world so much that he gave his only Son, so that everyone who believes in him may not die but have eternal life.

John 3:16

11 PEACE IN OUR WORLD

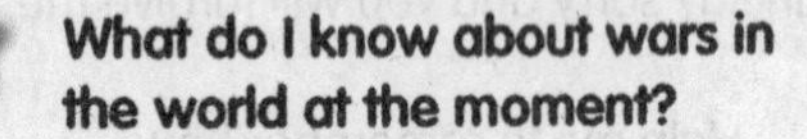

What do I know about wars in the world at the moment?

What might people be scared of?

What might give them hope?

PRAYER

Dear Jesus,
there always seems to be something
in the news about war.
I am thankful that there isn't war in my country.

Please be with the people who live with war.
Please give them something to hope for.

Please help the leaders of those countries
to try to work for peace
so the people can feel safe.

Amen

BIBLE VERSE

He sets the time for love and the time for hate,
the time for war and the time for peace.

Ecclesiastes 3:8

12 SEEING GOOD IN OTHERS

What good can I see in my brother (or sister!)?

What good can I see in my friends?

What good do I want them to see in me?

PRAYER

Dear Jesus,
please help me to remember to look at
what kind of person someone is,
rather than just what kind of stuff they have.

Thank you that you see who we are as people
and want to help us grow into
who you want us to be.
Amen

BIBLE VERSE

Above everything, love one another earnestly,
because love covers over many sins.

1 Peter 4:8